Back to School

Maya Ajmera • John D. Ivanko

with a foreword by Dr. Marilyn Jachetti Whirry
National Teacher of the Year

SHAKTI for Children

 Charlesbridge

Education is a wonderful adventure. It starts when you are a small child and lasts the rest of your life. My own journey into learning began on my first day of school. I made a mistake and went to a first grade classroom. Three weeks later, someone discovered that I should have been in kindergarten. But it was too late! I had already caught the excitement of learning, the joy of discovery, and the pride of being independent. So I stayed in first grade, and I loved it!

Going to school opens your mind to learning about different cultures, ideas, and people. At school you find out about all the wonders of the universe, and you learn to understand them. No matter what kind of school you go to, your teachers give you the greatest gifts of all: the freedom to learn and to dream and to succeed. With these gifts, you can be anything.

—Dr. Marilyn Jachetti Whirry
National Teacher of the Year 2000

Going to school means learning

Visiting an art museum in Mexico

about the world around you.

Sharing a book with a classmate in Pakistan

Sketching a standing stone in the United Kingdom

There are many kinds of schools

Taking notes in Australia

Having class outside in Mali

Attending night school in India

Being home-schooled in France

and lots of ways to get to them.

Riding on a horse-drawn wagon in Bolivia

Climbing onto a school bus in the United States

Traveling by boat in Peru

Squeezing onto a rickshaw in the Philippines

You might wear a uniform

Lining up for class in South Africa

Listening to the teacher in Thailand

or your favorite outfit.

Creating an art project in Belgium

Walking to school with a friend in France

When you are at school, you learn

*Forming words on a
slate in Bangladesh*

*Writing a story
in Niger*

to read and write

Studying the
alphabet in Rwanda

Writing on the chalkboard
in Saudi Arabia

and count and experiment.

*Adding numbers
in Algeria*

*Conducting lab
experiments in Mexico*

Counting with number cubes in Rwanda

School is for discovering science

Examining an atlas in the United States

Researching a science project in Trinidad and Tobago

and geography and language

Listening to a language tape in China

Hearing new words in Russia

and for developing physical

*Exercising in the
schoolyard in Iraq*

*Drawing a picture
in Bhutan*

fitness and artistic talent.

Practicing the violin in South Korea

At school you take field trips

Looking into a microscope at a science museum in the United States

Climbing on top of cannons at a fort in Cuba

and join teams and clubs.

Getting ready for a rugby match in New Zealand

Gathering for a club meeting in Syria

When you are a student, you learn

Gathering around the
teacher in the United States

Receiving help on homework
in Bangladesh

from many different people.

Learning sign language in South Africa

Getting together for group work in Nepal

You work hard on your lessons

*Jotting down
ideas in China*

*Taking notes
in South Africa*

*Working in the
computer lab in Israel*

*Learning to print
in Nepal*

and enjoy new challenges

Choosing books at the school library in the United States

Climbing rope ladders in the gymnasium in Russia

and make good friends.

*Telling a joke
in Bhutan*

*Sharing comic
books during
recess in France*

Going to school is loads of fun!

Answering questions in Iraq

Playing a board game in Canada

Goofing around after school in the Dominican Republic

WHERE YOU LEARN

No two schools are the same. Some schools have many rooms, others have just one room, and some hold classes at home or outside. Schools can be just for boys or just for girls or for boys and girls together. Students get to school in many ways: on foot, by bus, or even by boat. Whether your school is large or small, close by or far away, it is one of the best places to explore new ideas and discover why things work the way they do.

Trinidad and Tobago

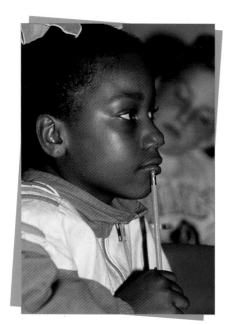

United States

HOW YOU LEARN

Every school day brings new challenges. You do some assignments on your own and work on others with your classmates. Field trips to museums or nature centers give you a chance to see things up close. Schools teach social studies, math, science, art, writing, music, and reading. These classes help you discover which subjects you like most and encourage you to think about what you want to be when you grow up.

WHO TEACHES YOU?

At school you discover new words, places, numbers, and faces. This can be hard work, but your teachers, family, and friends guide you and help you learn. Sometimes they tutor you or look over your homework. They also offer encouragement and support so you will succeed.

Austria

Bolivia

BEING A GOOD STUDENT

Knowing the answer to a tough question feels great. It takes lots of hard work and commitment. Writing well, counting correctly, and remembering important information are things you have to do on your own. School is also a place to learn how to be a good citizen and to help others in your community. Going to school is a big step toward growing up.

FRIENDSHIPS AND FUN

School is a great place to make friends and have fun. Through after-school activities like soccer, Scouts, or chess club you can meet other students who share your interests. In band, art, and gym classes you can enjoy developing new talents. Hanging out with friends, playing a game of tag, working with others on a class project, and sharing a secret over lunch are fun activities that are often full of laughter.

Japan

Back to School *is dedicated to the Christ School of the Bundibugyo District of Uganda.*
—M. A.

Dedicated to the "seventh generation of children on Earth."
—J. I.

I wish to thank Jack V. Matson, who is my favorite teacher; Jennifer Isern, who opened her home in D.C. to me during the creation of this book; David Ivanko, my brother and a great teacher; and my wife, Lisa Kivirist. It has been a wonderful creative partnership to work with Maya Ajmera and to share in her vision for what the world can become, one child at a time.
—*John Ivanko*

As always, my deepest thanks to John Ivanko.
—*Maya Ajmera*

We would both like to thank our fantastic editors, Kelly Swanson Turner and Lisa Laird; Charlesbridge Publishing; and Andy Drewlinger and Jon Quam of the National Teacher of the Year program.

Financial support for this project has been provided by the W. K. Kellogg Foundation and the Flora Family Foundation.

Back to School is a project of SHAKTI for Children, which is dedicated to teaching children to value diversity and to grow into productive and caring citizens of the world. SHAKTI for Children is a program of the Global Fund for Children, a non-profit organization. Visit www.globalfundforchildren.org to learn more about the Christ School in Uganda.

Published by Charlesbridge
85 Main Street, Watertown, MA 02472
(617) 926-0329 • www.charlesbridge.com

Developed by SHAKTI for Children
The Global Fund for Children
1101 Fourteenth Street, NW, Suite 420, Washington, DC 20005
(202) 331-9003 • www.shakti.org

Details about donation of royalties can be obtained by writing to Charlesbridge Publishing and the Global Fund for Children.

Other SHAKTI for Children/Charlesbridge Books
Children from Australia to Zimbabwe: A Photographic Journey around the World by Maya Ajmera and Anna Rhesa Versola
Come Out and Play by Maya Ajmera and John Ivanko
Extraordinary Girls by Maya Ajmera, Olateju Omolodun, and Sarah Strunk
Let the Games Begin! by Maya Ajmera and Michael J. Regan
To Be a Kid by Maya Ajmera and John Ivanko
Xanadu, the Imaginary Place: A Showcase of Writings and Artwork by North Carolina's Children edited by Maya Ajmera and Olateju Omolodun

Library of Congress Cataloging-in-Publication Data
Ajmera, Maya.
Back to school/Maya Ajmera, John Ivanko.
    p.   cm.
    ISBN-13: 978-1-57091-383-9 (reinforced for library use)
    ISBN-10: 1-57091-383-8 (reinforced for library use)
    ISBN-13: 978-1-57091-384-6 (softcover)
    ISBN-10: 1-57091-384-6 (softcover)
1. Education, Elementary—Juvenile literature. 2. Elementary schools—Juvenile literature. [1. Schools. 2. Education.]
I. Ivanko, John D. (John Duane), 1966- . II. Shakti for Children (Organization). III. Title.
LB1556.A56   2001
372—dc21   00-064328

Printed in South Korea
(hc) 10 9 8 7 6 5 4 3 2
(sc) 10 9 8 7 6 5 4 3

Cover photograph from Tibet (China)
Title page photograph from Ecuador
Page 2 photograph from the United States
Backcover photograph from South Africa

Display type and text type set in Jacoby, Stone Serif, and Stone Sans
Scans produced by Sung In Printing, South Korea
Color separations made by Sung In Printing, South Korea
Printed and bound by Sung In Printing, South Korea
Production supervision by Brian G. Walker
Designed by Diane M. Earley

Photographs: (left to right and top to bottom):
Cover: © Jeffrey Aaronson/Network Aspen; Front flap of the hardcover: © Katrina Thomas/Aramco World; Title page: © Elaine Little; p. 2: © Kathleen Burke/Aramco World; p. 4: © Stephanie Maze/Woodfin Camp; p. 5: © 2000 Jon Warren, © John D. Ivanko; p. 6: © Robert Frerck/Woodfin Camp, © Nik Wheeler; p. 7: © Monkmeyer/Sidney, © 2000 Jon Warren; p. 8: © John D. Ivanko, © 2000 Jon Warren; p. 9: © Nik Wheeler, © Katsuyoshi Tanaka/Woodfin Camp; p. 10: © Elaine Little, © Nik Wheeler; p. 11: © Stephanie Maze/Woodfin Camp, © Elaine Little; p. 12: © 2000 Jon Warren, © S. Noorani/Woodfin Camp; p. 13: © Betty Press/Woodfin Camp, © Katrina Thomas/Aramco World; p. 14: © Sean Sprague, © Anne B. Keiser; p. 15: © Betty Press/ Woodfin Camp, © Nik Wheeler; p. 16: © Betty Press/Woodfin Camp; p. 17: © Mike Yamashita/Woodfin Camp, © Monkmeyer/Siteman; p. 18: © Nik Wheeler, © 2000 Jon Warren; p. 19: © Stephanie Maze/ Woodfin Camp; p. 20: © Richard Nowitz, © Nik Wheeler; p. 21: © Nik Wheeler, © Kevin Fleming/Woodfin Camp; p. 22: © Monkmeyer/Byron, © 2000 Jon Warren; p. 23: © Elaine Little, © 2000 Jon Warren; p. 24: © Elaine Little, © Stephanie Maze/Woodfin Camp; p. 25: © Nik Wheeler, © 2000 Jon Warren; p. 26: © Monkmeyer/Kerbs, © Mike Yamashita/Woodfin Camp; p. 27: © 2000 Jon Warren, © Monkmeyer /Rogers; p. 28: © John Eastcott/Yva Momatiuk/Woodfin Camp; p. 29: © Monkmeyer/Bopp; p. 30: © Betty Press/Woodfin Camp, © Elaine Little; p. 31: © Monkmeyer/Conklin, © 2000 Jon Warren, © Monkmeyer/Hasegawa; Back cover of the hardcover: © Elaine Little.